W9-AYK-891

The Reptile Class

Family Trees

The Reptile Class

MARC ZABLUDOFF

 **Marshall Cavendish**
Benchmark
New York

Marshall Cavendish Benchmark
99 White Plains Road
Tarrytown, New York 10591-9001
www.marshallcavendish.us

Library of Congress Cataloging-in-Publication Data

Zabludoff, Marc.
The reptile class / by Marc Zabludoff.
p. cm. — (Family trees)
Includes bibliographical references (p.   ) and index.
ISBN 0-7614-1820-2
1. Reptiles—Juvenile literature. I. Title. II. Series.

QL644.2.Z33 2005
597.9—dc22
2004021820

Front cover: A green sea turtle
Title page: A frilled lizard
Back cover: *Brookesia minima,* the world's smallest chameleon
Photo research by Linda Sykes Picture Research
The photographs in this book are used by permission and through the courtesy of: Stephen Frink/Corbis: front
cover; Frans Lanting/Minden Pictures: back cover, 10 left, 52, 64, 67; Leo Meier/Corbis: 3, 70; Natural History
Museum, London: 6; Jim Merli/Visuals Unlimited: 10 right, 40; Sunset Photo Agency/Animals, Animals - Earth
Scenes: 12; Heide and Hans Jurgen Koch/Minden Pictures: 13; Keith Eskanos/Picturequest: 14 top right;
Picturequest: 14 middle left; Burke/Triolo/Picturequest: 14 middle left; Jeff Schultz/Alaskan Express/Picturequest:
12 middle right; Martin Ruegner/Imagestate-Pictor/Picturequest: 15 bottom middle; Royalty-Free/Corbis: 14 top
left; 14 middle center, 14 bottom left, 15 top right, 15 middle row (all), 15 bottom left; David Dennis/Animals
Animals/Earth Scenes: 15 top left Sea World, Inc./ Corbis: 14 bottom right Swift/Vanuga Images/Corbis: 14 bottom
row (middle); Photodisc/Getty Images: 14 bottom right, 15 bottom row, second from right, 15 bottom right; M.
Kulyk/Photo Researchers, Inc.: 16; Louie Psihoyos/Corbis: 22, 25; Lawrence Lawry/Photo Researchers, Inc.: 24; Joe
McDonald/Visuals Unlimited: 28, 60, 62; ZSSDI/Minden Pictures: 30; Gerry Ellis/Minden Pictures: 32; James
Steinberg/Photo Researchers, Inc.: 33; Fred Bavendam/Minden Pictures: 36; Mike Parry/Minden Pictures: 38;
Stephen Dalton/Photo Researchers, Inc.: 42, 43; SATeam/Foto Natura/Minden Pictures: 45; Fred
Whitehead/Animals, Animals - Earth Scenes: 47; Art Wolfe/Photo Researchers, Inc.: 48; Breck Kent/Animals
Animals - Earth Scenes: 50; S. K. Patrick/Visuals Unlimited: 51; Zigmund Leszczynski/ Animals Animals - Earth
Scenes: 53; Alison Wright/Corbis: 54; Sunset Photo Agency/Animals, Animals - Earth Scenes: 55; George H. H.
Huey/Animals, Animals - Earth Scenes: 58; Michael Dick/Animals, Animals - Earth Scenes: 65; OSF/Deeble &
Stone/Animals, Animals - Earth Scenes: 68; Raymond Mendez/Animals, Animals - Earth Scenes: 72; Daniel
Heuclin/Photo Researchers, Inc.: 73; Michael and Patricia Fogden/Minden Pictures: 74; N. Bromhall/ OSF/Animals,
Animals - Earth Scenes: 76; Lynda Richardson/Corbis: 78; Keren Su/Corbis: 79; Gerald & Buff Corsi/Visuals
Unlimited: 80; John Cancalosi/Peter Arnold: 81; Tui de Roy/ Minden Pictures: 82.

Printed in Malaysia

Book design by Patrice Sheridan

1 3 5 6 4 2

C O N T E N T S

By 1917, when this *Iguanodon* was found, scientists knew that a dinosaur's legs were not splayed out like a lizard's. But they still showed its tail dragging on the ground.

Making Orders

In 1822 a woman named Mary Ann Mantell pulled some odd-looking teeth from a pile of stones in southern England and helped to rewrite the history of the world. Not all at once, and not all by herself, but she did get things going. Mary Ann was the wife of Gideon Algernon Mantell, a country doctor and a passionate observer of nature. The teeth, he noted, were brown, chisel-shaped, very old, and very long. Except for their great length, he thought, they rather resembled the teeth of an iguana, a medium-size lizard.

Eventually, Dr. Mantell's notion was confirmed by the leading scientists of his day, and the unknown animal to which the teeth once belonged was given the name *Iguanodon,* meaning "iguana tooth." It was the first dinosaur ever named, and the first hint that once upon a time, giant reptiles had roamed the earth.

As more fossil discoveries soon showed, *Iguanodon* was a huge creature, stretching 33 feet (10 m) from snout to tail. It had two enormous hind legs and two smaller front legs, and it used its large teeth for chomping on plants. It was nothing like any reptile that scientists of the day knew about—not like any lizard or snake or turtle or crocodile. Yet the scientists had no doubt that *Iguanodon* was indeed a reptile. The teeth told them so.

The evidence they relied on had been gathered over the preceding century and a half by several scientists, beginning with an Englishman named John Ray (1627-1705). More than a hundred years before the first dinosaur teeth were identified, Ray had led the first scientific effort to make some sense out of the bewildering jumble of life-forms he found all around him.

Today we take a lot of our knowledge about the world for granted. We learn that although bats fly, they are not birds, and that although whales swim in the sea, they are not fish. But people were not always so clear as to what characteristics properly place an animal in one group rather than another—bats and whales with mammals, for instance, rather than with birds and fish.

The natural world can seem a very messy playroom. Animals come in all sorts of designs. Some have wings, some have fins; some have bones, some are mere jelly; some have two legs, others four, five, six, eight, ten, and more. Humans have always tried to find some order in the mishmash of body types. But then, we seem to be driven to organize things of all sorts. At the very least, order helps us find something when we need it: words in a dictionary, books in a library, matching socks in a drawer.

But books and socks are relatively easy to sort. Nature is harder. Do dogs and cats belong together since they both make good pets? How about cats and catfish—do their whiskers make them as good a pair as, say, sea lions and lions? What about eels and snakes, or salamanders and lizards? What are the rules that tell us who belongs where?

For two thousand years before Ray, people had come up with various methods for arranging the inhabitants of the living world. Some stressed the animals' importance to people, putting "valuable" animals like dogs and chickens together, for example. Some stressed instead an animal's character, putting the "noble" lion in one group, the "lowly" hyena in another. Still others stressed the animal's natural home, for example, putting together all creatures of the sea.

FROM RAY TO LINNAEUS

Ray was one of the first people to study the small details of animal bodies, looking for features that some animals shared and others did not. Among the things he found most revealing were hooves and toes and teeth. Ray did not know why these features were so important. Neither he nor anyone else at the time suspected that some animals might have the same kind of teeth because they inherited them from the same ancestors. And they certainly did not suspect that these ancestors might have lived hundreds of millions of years earlier. If goats and sheep resembled each other in feet and teeth, Ray thought, it was a sign that God had imposed a hidden order on the natural world. If he could decipher that order, he could better understand God's lesson for humankind.

Ray published a catalog in 1693 describing hundreds of animals and noting their similarities and differences. Decades later, Ray's work was hugely enlarged by the Swedish scientist Karl von Linné (1707-1778), or Linnaeus, as he is usually known. Linnaeus described several thousand more animals, and in far more detail. Linnaeus arranged all the animals in appropriate groups, based on their physical similarities. Most importantly, he also came up with the method of naming plants and animals that we still use today.

Linnaeus, like Ray, started with the observation that animals were divided into a large number of distinct types that always produced descendants just like themselves. Wolves, it was clear, always produced new wolves, never weasels. These basic types he called species. Different species, however, were sometimes very similar to each other. Horses and zebras, for example, are quite alike in general appearance and structure, despite their obvious differences. Such similar species, Linnaeus reasoned, belonged together in a broader category, which he called a genus.

Linnaeus gave names to all the species and genera (plural of *genus*) he identified, but he did not give them Swedish names. He named them all

The Galapagos giant tortoise and the five-lined skink represent two very different, but related, orders within the class Reptilia.

in Latin, the common language of scholars everywhere in Europe. Difficulty in communication was a serious problem for scientists. Not only did languages differ, but even in a single language people often had different names for the same animal. Even today, one person's woodchuck is another's groundhog. Scientists of the eighteenth century could never be absolutely certain that anyone else knew precisely which animal they were talking about. What they needed, Linnaeus knew, were agreed-upon *scientific* names.

The genus and species name together did the trick. An animal assigned to its proper two categories could be given a first name (its genus) and a last name (its species) that would distinguish it from all others, even very similar animals. For example, all dogs and wolves belong to the same genus, *Canis;* and so both dogs and wolves have the same first name. Dogs are further identified by their species name, *familiaris;* wolves are further identified by the species name *lupus.* (By tradition, genus names are capitalized while species names are lowercased, and both are written in italics). The two animals are shown by their names to be similar, but different. *Canis familiaris* makes a good sheep-watcher. *Canis lupus* makes a good sheep-eater.

FROM LINNAEUS TO TODAY

Linnaeus and later scientists added broader categories to the system. Groups of similar genera were collected into a family. Similar families were collected into an order, similar orders into a class. Each of these categories was called a taxon, and so the science of classification became known as taxonomy. At the very highest level, classes were collected into a phylum, and phyla (plural of *phylum*) into a kingdom.

Linnaeus placed animals into their various slots based purely on the way they looked. Today, we have other standards that help us decide in which group an animal belongs—among them are details of the animal's DNA, inside its cells. We want our categories to show not just which animals look most alike, but also which animals are most closely related. In other words, we want to show how animals have evolved, or changed from their shared ancestors, over many millions of years.

Most scientists agree that there are five kingdoms of life: animals, plants, fungi, bacteria, and protoctists (mostly single-celled organisms). There is some disagreement on how many phyla there are, but somewhere around thirty in the animal kingdom. A phylum represents a basic body plan that is fundamentally different from all others. Earthworms are in one phylum, for instance, while starfish are in another.

Gathered into those phyla of animals are dozens of classes. Reptiles, along with fish, amphibians, birds, and mammals, represent classes in the phylum with which we are most familiar—the chordates, or animals that have spinal chords. (Most chordates also have backbones, or vertebrae, and are known as vertebrates.) Within the reptile class, a particular animal is identified further with labels for its order, family, and so on.

Chondropython viridis, commonly known as the green tree python. As the snake matures, its color will change from yellow to green.

Classifying Life

Here is a classification for a common resident of Florida, the American alligator (*Alligator mississippiensis*):

Kingdom	Animalia (all the animals)
Phylum	Chordata (all animals with a spinal cord)
Class	Reptilia (all the reptiles)
Order	Crocodylia (all crocodiles, alligators, caimans, and gharials)
Family	Alligatoridae (alligators and caimans)
Genus	*Alligator* (alligators)
Species	*mississippiensis* (American alligator)

Scientists classify living things in arrangements like this family tree of the anim

A N I M A L

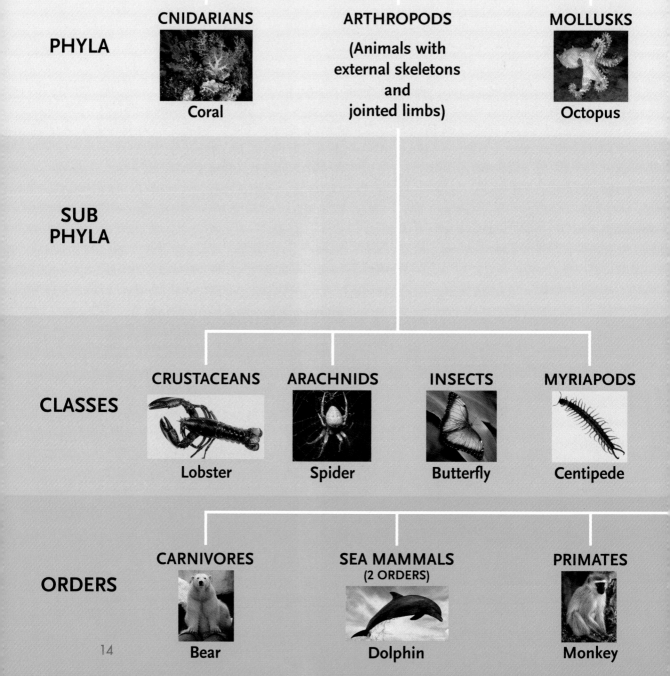

PHYLA

CNIDARIANS

Coral

ARTHROPODS

(Animals with
external skeletons
and
jointed limbs)

MOLLUSKS

Octopus

**SUB
PHYLA**

CLASSES

CRUSTACEANS

Lobster

ARACHNIDS

Spider

INSECTS

Butterfly

MYRIAPODS

Centipede

ORDERS

CARNIVORES

Bear

SEA MAMMALS
(2 ORDERS)

Dolphin

PRIMATES

Monkey

ngdom to highlight the connections and the differences among the many forms of life.

KINGDOM

ANNELIDS

Earthworm

CHORDATES

(Animals
with a
dorsal
nerve chord)

ECHINODERMS

Starfish

VERTEBRATES

(Animals
with a
backbone)

FISH

Fish

BIRDS

Penguin

MAMMALS

AMPHIBIANS

Frog

REPTILES

Snake

HERBIVORES
(5 ORDERS)

Horse

RODENTS

Squirrel

INSECTIVORES

Hedgehog

MARSUPIALS

Kangaroo

SMALL MAMMALS
(SEVERAL ORDERS)

Rabbit

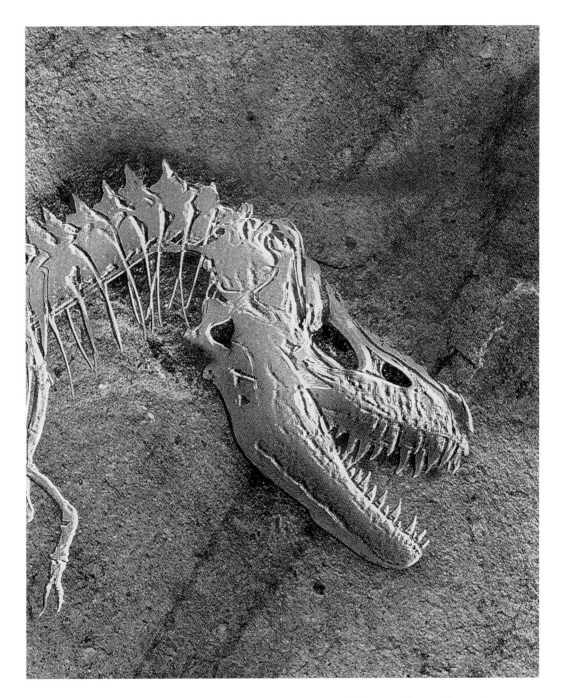

As dinosaurs, reptiles appeared in some of their most diverse, and fearsome, forms. This *Tarbosaurus*, a *T. rex* relative, lived 75 million years ago in central Asia

Reptile History

Reptiles, along with all amphibians (frogs, toads, and salamanders), birds, and mammals, are part of the great collection of creatures known as tetrapods, or "four-footed" animals. The group includes such animals as whales, snakes, bats, and others that may have lost two or more of their four limbs or changed them into something else—wings or fins—more suitable for their lifestyle.

The tetrapod story began around 370 million years ago, when a group of fish began to crawl out of the water, at least for short periods. Over time, the descendants of these fish gradually developed proper lungs, legs, shoulders and hips, and strong muscles that could lift their bodies up off the ground. The first true tetrapods were amphibians, like today's frogs. They did not look anything like frogs—they were more lizard-like, with four sprawling legs, a tail, and a snout. But, like frogs, they were fully able to live on land, except for one detail—to reproduce, they had to return to the water and behave like their fishy ancestors. Amphibians have no choice in this. Their jelly-like eggs, if laid on land, will dry out and die. Also, the young animals that hatch out of those eggs are not ready for life on land. Amphibian eggs are small, and the babies do not develop completely inside them. When the eggs hatch, the animal that emerges is in an immature form, suited only for life underwater. A tadpole is a perfect example. More fish than frog, it must stay in the water for a period of growth and development before it can take up residence on land.

It might seem that early amphibians would have been better off staying in the water. But they had good reasons for moving. There were far fewer predators on land, for one thing. And there was an abundance of food: an inexhaustible meal of insects and spiders, whose ancestors had come onto the land tens of millions of years earlier. Any animals that could make use of the land's shelter and food had a pretty good chance of success—"success" meaning that they could thrive and leave many off-spring to carry on their legacy. Early amphibians were indeed successful. Still, their dependence on the water meant that they could never stray too far inland.

Several hundred million years ago, there was a lot of land inland. Back then, Earth was a very different place from the planet we know now. All the continents were in different spots on the globe. They were not sep-arated by broad oceans, but were instead all joined together in one huge "supercontinent" known as Pangaea. This enormous landmass, stretching nearly from pole to pole, naturally had a vast interior, away from the sea. Compared with the coast, this inner land was hot and dry—completely unsuitable for an amphibian, but a tremendous opportunity for any ani-mals able to survive there.

A NEW EGG

Some animals were soon able to take advantage of this strange land, thanks to the development of a new kind of egg. Unlike amphibian eggs, this new egg was large and encased in a waterproof covering that kept it from drying out easily. This tough outer shell allowed gases like oxygen to flow through but kept fluids inside from evaporating. Within the egg, a skin-like membrane enclosed the embryo (the developing baby) in a fluid-filled sac. Another membrane surrounded and protected a large yolk (the food supply for the embryo). The larger size of the egg and the bigger food supply meant that the baby within could develop much more fully. It no longer had to go through a "tadpole" stage and could pop out of the egg ready to function on land.

The membrane surrounding the embryo in this egg is called the amnion, and the egg is called an amniotic egg. The evolution of the amniotic egg was a critical event in life's history. Animals that laid such eggs could seek out territories far from the sea. They could live in areas and feast on foods that were unavailable to the amphibians.

A huge variety of new animals soon evolved. From these amniotic-egg-laying creatures—or amniotes—eventually came all the reptiles living today. These include the snakes and lizards, the crocodiles and alligators, the tortoises and the turtles. So too came all the great reptiles that are now extinct: all the dinosaurs, all the flying pterosaurs, all the swimming ichthyosaurs. Those early amniotes eventually produced all the birds and—of special interest to us humans—all the mammals. We are all the lucky result of that Earth-changing event, the development of the amniotic egg.

Amniotes rapidly "conquered" the land and developed into three main groups: anapsids, synapsids, and diapsids. Today, strange as it may sound, we can distinguish the fossils of each group by the holes in their heads—more precisely, by openings in the sides of their skulls just behind the eye sockets.

THE AGE OF REPTILES

The oldest fossil we have of a reptile-like animal is around 340 million years old. The creature is called *Westlothiana lizziae* and known to scientists the world over as Lizzie. Whether Lizzie was a true reptile is a matter of

Holey Heads

- Anapsids had no skull openings at all. In this, they resembled amphibians and fish. Their skulls were solid bony cases, well built for armored protection. Among today's reptiles, only turtles have this skull design.

- Synapsids had a single opening low down on the side of the skull. This was the most popular skull model among early amniotes, and many sported a synapsid head at the end of their neck. These animals are often called the mammal-like reptiles because after 100 million years or so they did indeed evolve into mammals. The synapsids themselves are all long extinct.

- Diapsids had two skull openings behind the eye, and many of them are extinct also. Others are very much alive, though—except for the turtles, all today's reptiles have diapsid skulls. These modern diapsids are usually further divided into two groups: the lepidosaurs and the archosaurs. In the first group are all the snakes and lizards, along with a few others (the worm-lizards and tuataras). The archosaurs (which means "ruling reptiles") is made up today only of crocodilians—crocodiles, alligators, caimans, and the gharial. But once upon a time it included all the land-roaming dinosaurs and the high-flying pterosaurs. Technically, since birds evolved from dinosaurs, they too are archosaurs—reptiles with feathers.

What purpose did these holey heads serve? There seem to be two possibilities. One is that the holes allowed the animal's skull to stay strong but to weigh less. The second possibility is that the holes opened up some room for bigger muscles that were moving ever more powerful jaws.

REPTILE SKULLS

ANAPSID

SYNAPSID

DIAPSID

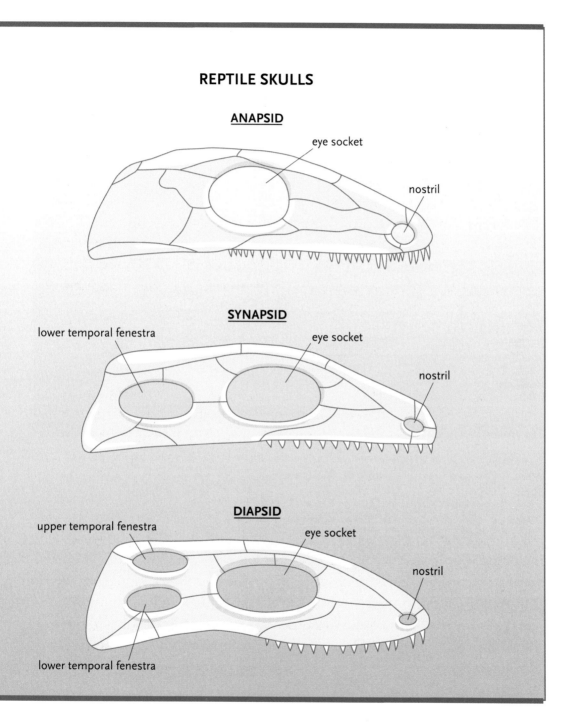

A model shows a baby dinosaur curled up inside its amniotic egg. The egg kept the embryo from drying out and enabled reptiles to live far from the sea.

ongoing debate. But most paleontologists—scientists who study ancient life—agree that reptiles began to evolve around this time, give or take a few tens of millions of years. Early reptiles were small, slender animals, perhaps 8 inches (20 cm) or so long. From the beginning they were equipped with sharp teeth, and they were probably eager eaters of insects. The oldest fossils of undisputed reptiles were found trapped inside the fossilized remains of hollowed-out tree trunks. Apparently, the animals had come into the trunks to dine on insects that were themselves feasting on the rotting wood.

If we were making a movie of amniote history, for the next 100 million years we would focus not on the diapsids, which would become true reptiles, but on the synapsids, the mammal-like reptiles. The diapsids had to wait a bit before taking center stage. But when they did, they did it in a spectacular manner.

We humans have a compulsion for making categories, especially when it comes to science. We sort not only living animals and plants into different categories but fossil animals and plants also, and we arrange Earth's history into different categories based on the age of the fossils we find. One of these categories is called the Mesozoic era. Mesozoic means "middle time," and it is the span of years between the Paleozoic ("ancient time") and the Cenozoic ("modern time"). It was a long stretch: more than 180 million years, from about 248 million years ago to 65 million years ago. To make it manageable, we break the Mesozoic era into three smaller periods: the Triassic, the Jurassic, and the Cretaceous. Together these periods make up a time that is nearly always referred to as the Age of Reptiles.

Reptiles began appearing in a staggering variety of forms. During the Triassic, around 245 million years ago, some reptiles returned to the sea, much as the mammal ancestors of whales and dolphins would do later. There they developed into the toothy predators called ichthyosaurs and long-necked, Loch Ness monster look-alikes called plesiosaurs.

On land, other fearsome predators appeared: the ancestors of today's crocodiles and alligators. One of these ancient crocs, called *Deinosuchus,* was a terrifying 36-foot (11 m), six-ton predator with a lower jaw 6 feet (1.8 m) long. At the same time, other reptiles were developing into dinosaurs, among which were the largest land animals Earth has ever known.

The air too became busy with new animals as still another group of reptiles started developing extremely long finger bones and stretching wings made of skin between the bones. These animals, the pterosaurs, would dominate the skies until the spread of yet another reptile offshoot, the feathered birds.

During the Age of Reptiles, long-necked plesiosaurs swam the seas with flipper-like feet. But they developed from animals that once walked on land.

Turtles also got their start during the Triassic, and they too tried out large sizes for a while—one reached a length of 12 feet (3.7 m). Lizards came a bit later, around 185 million years ago. Snakes, which most likely evolved from one group of burrowing lizards, appeared much more recently—100 million years ago or so. But as even this very condensed story of reptile evolution shows, all of today's reptiles share a very old and glorious history.

THE END OF AN AGE

For many of the ancient reptiles, that history ended with the great extinction at the end of the Cretaceous. Many others animals disappeared then also. Some vanished suddenly, while others had already been dwindling for a long time. But by 65 million years ago, all the dinosaurs were gone from the land, the ichthyosaurs and the plesiosaurs no longer patrolled the seas, and the pterosaurs had left the skies clear for the birds. With them went a number of other reptile groups. Among the turtles, for example, seven of the fifteen families went extinct. On the other hand, whatever killed off the dinosaurs—and

Was *Archaeopteryx* a bird with teeth or a dinosaur with feathers? This famous fossil presents strong evidence that birds evolved from one line of dinosaurs.

most scientists believe that an asteroid or meteor hitting Earth was in some way involved—hardly affected the crocodiles at all.

The millions of years since the end of the Mesozoic have not been kind to reptiles, overall. During their heyday, there were seventeen reptile orders. Today there are only four. But even though they no longer appear in forms as widely distinctive as pterodactyls and tyrannosaurs, reptiles still show up in a confusing variety of shapes and sizes. And they still appear in many more forms than we mammals do. There are some 8,000 reptile species and only 4,600 mammal species.

Taxonomists have gathered those reptile species into more than 1,000 genera, 58 families, and the four existing orders of the class Reptilia. Those orders, reflecting the different lines of ancestry, are:

- Testudines, which includes all turtles and tortoises (*tortoise,* by the way, is a name that means different things to different people, but in the United States it usually refers to large land-dwelling turtles);
- Crocodylia, which includes not only crocodiles but also alligators, the caimans of Central and South America, and the gharial of northern India, Pakistan, Bangladesh, and Nepal;
- Squamata, which includes all the snakes, the lizards, and the group of burrowing creatures known as worm-lizards;
- Rhynchocephalia, an ancient order represented today only by the two species of lizardlike but distinct tuataras, which live only on a few dozen islands around New Zealand.

The thousands of species these orders hold may not match the overwhelming variety of reptiles that flourished in the ancient past, but they are still impressive. And they are different enough from each other that it is often quite difficult to talk about them as one group of animals at all.

REPTILE TIMELINE

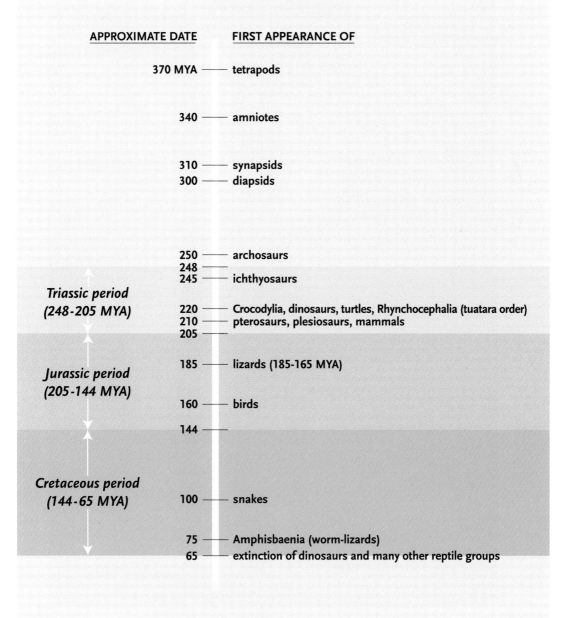

APPROXIMATE DATE	FIRST APPEARANCE OF
370 MYA	tetrapods
340	amniotes
310	synapsids
300	diapsids
250	archosaurs
248	
245	ichthyosaurs
220	Crocodylia, dinosaurs, turtles, Rhynchocephalia (tuatara order)
210	pterosaurs, plesiosaurs, mammals
205	
185	lizards (185-165 MYA)
160	birds
144	
100	snakes
75	Amphisbaenia (worm-lizards)
65	extinction of dinosaurs and many other reptile groups

*Triassic period
(248-205 MYA)*

*Jurassic period
(205-144 MYA)*

*Cretaceous period
(144-65 MYA)*

MYA = million years ago

The tokay gecko is a typical, small, insect-eating reptile. But it is not immediately apparent what features it shares with other reptiles such as crocodiles and turtles.

CHAPTER **T W O**

The Reptile Body

With features ranging from turtle shells to snaky forked tongues, reptiles are not easily described as a group. Yet there are some common features that set reptiles apart from other animals and link them together.

SCALY SKIN

The reptiles' most significant feature is their scaly skin. A reptile's skin is built in layers, the outermost of which is made of a protein called keratin. Keratin is a common substance in animal bodies. It comes in two forms; one is hard and stiff, while the other is soft and flexible. The hard form shows up in such animal features as fingernails. The soft form appears in such adornments as hair.

Reptiles have an abundance of both forms. One makes the hard, tough slabs that we call scales. The other is found between the scales, in small, flexible connecting sections that allow the toughened skin to bend.

The scaly skin seals in moisture and protects the body from the drying effects of the environment. It also gives reptiles some protection against

29

A young armadillo girdled lizard protects its vulnerable belly by curling up and biting its tail, offering only a mouthful of spiky scales to any predator.

predators. That protection is often reinforced by bones. Turtles, crocodilians, and some lizards have plates of bone embedded in the inner layer of their skin, beneath the scales. These plates, called osteoderms, are loosely connected to one another and lie directly below the toughest scales on the body. On a crocodile's back, for example, parallel rows of bony plates run beneath the thick hard scales on the surface, creating a body armor that cannot be pierced.

A turtle's shell too is a combination of scales and bone, completely inseparable from the rest of the animal. Unlike the image we might get from cartoons, the shell of a turtle is not a detachable container that merely encloses an otherwise naked animal. Rather it is literally the skin and bones that form the back and front of the animal's body.

A turtle's shell is built in layers. The outside is made of enlarged scales, which are often called scutes. The inside is made of 40 to 60 pieces of bone that lie within the skin. These bones are fused, or joined, to the turtle's backbone and ribs on top and to the ribs and shoulder bones on the bottom. (The top half of the shell is called the carapace; the bottom is called the plastron.) The two halves of the shell are joined by more pieces of bone that form "bridges" along the sides. Not all turtles, by the way, have hard shells. In some "softshell" species the shell has become less bony and more leathery.

All reptile groups modify, or change, the scales on parts of their bodies for specific purposes. Many lizards have scales along their backs and

TURTLE SKELETON

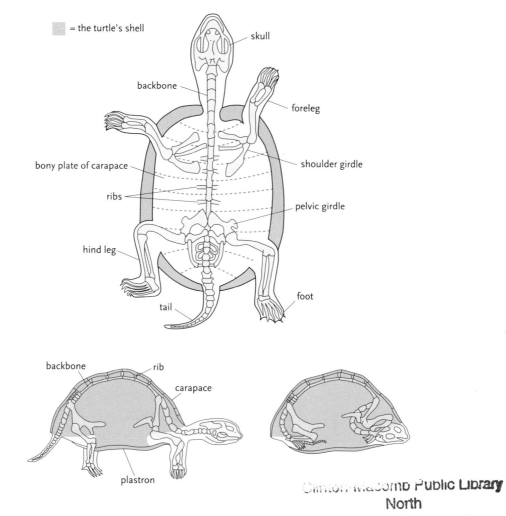

= the turtle's shell

skull

backbone

foreleg

bony plate of carapace

shoulder girdle

ribs

pelvic girdle

hind leg

foot

tail

backbone   rib

carapace

plastron

The scales on a gecko's toes are divided into thousands of microscopic ridges that enable the lizard to cling to any vertical surface—even glass.

heads that grow into long crests or frills, often to impress members of the opposite sex. Some lizards have scales that grow into long hard spikes that make them look formidable to rivals and perhaps inedible to predators.

The remarkable climbing lizards known as geckos have scales on their feet that have been divided into thousands of microscopic ridges. They act as suction cups to let a gecko run up even a sheet of glass. Snakes generally have wide, overlapping scales on their undersides that push against the ground and allow the body to move forward. Burrowing worm-lizards have toughened scales on their snouts that let them dig their way into the ground.

A reptile's skin, though tough, is subjected to a fair amount of abuse, and so reptiles routinely replace their worn out skin with a new one. Snakes generally shed their skin in one piece, while lizards typically shed in large patches. Crocodilians and turtles just wear their skin away bit by bit, as we do. The scutes of a turtle's shell may or may not be shed, depending on the species.

EXTERNAL HEATING

What else do all reptiles have in common besides their scaly skin? Importantly, they are all "cold-blooded." That does not mean that they are cold. Actually, reptiles prefer to be on the hot side. Scientists prefer to use the term "ectothermic" to describe reptiles' metabolism. It means that, unlike mammals and birds, they do not use energy from food to keep their bodies at a constant temperature. Instead, they bask in the sun to warm up or retire to shady nooks or burrows to cool down. This takes up a lot of their time. But it also means that they do not spend a lot of their time eating—they do not eat nearly as much food as "endothermic" mammals or birds do to get all the energy they need.

Reptiles such as this spiny lizard in Utah are superbly adapted for desert life: they soak up heat from the sun, use very little energy, and recycle nearly all their moisture.

A VARIETY OF BODIES

Once we get past the skin, the bodies of reptiles begin to differ greatly. Turtles, for example, are the only animals that have their shoulder and hip bones inside their rib cage—a weird arrangement that became necessary as the ribs gradually joined with the shell. Snakes, in contrast, have mostly gotten rid of their shoulders and hips entirely. But snakes are hardly bone-less. As they have lost limbs, they have added vertebrae, or backbones. A snake may have hundreds of vertebrae, with hundreds of pairs of ribs attached to them. The snake's skeleton, very unlike the turtle's, is extremely flexible.

The mouths of reptiles in general are designed for grabbing and piercing, and sometimes for ripping. But reptiles do not go in much for chewing. Except for a handful of lizards and some tortoises, reptiles are meat eaters that swallow their prey whole, or in large chunks. Turtles do their chomping with jaws that are lined with a hard, sharp cutting edge made of keratin. Other reptiles, though, including most snakes, have teeth. In snakes, curved, backward-pointing teeth pull prey into the mouth. In crocodiles and alligators, large pointed teeth propelled by massive jaw muscles punch through meat and bones easily. Tuataras have a unique arrangement of teeth: a double row of them in the upper jaw, which forms a groove for the single row of teeth on the lower jaw. Unlike us, all reptiles replace their teeth continuously, throughout their entire lives.

Inside the body, the organs of reptiles are typical of land animals, with a few exceptions. Because reptiles do not chew their food, they usually have very muscular stomachs for breaking and crushing their food into small bits. Crocodilians, which often gulp down huge chunks of meat, have the largest stomach muscles.

Leading away from those stomachs are intestines, usually simple ones, as in all meat-eaters. Some large plant-eating tortoises have longer, more complicated intestines because plants are harder to digest. The intestines carry away waste to a chamber called the cloaca, which is found not

A crocodilian's skeleton plays an important part in its unusual movement. Ball-and-socket connections in the vertebrae give the animal great flexibility while swimming. Ankle joints allow it to twist all four feet forward, bring its legs close to the body, and walk upright, nearly like a mammal.

only in reptiles but also in amphibians and birds. The cloaca, at the base of the tail, is where wastes from both the intestines (feces) and the kidneys (urine) are discharged. It is also the spot where the reproductive organs are located.

For breathing, all reptiles are equipped with lungs. Like whales or walruses, even sea turtles and sea snakes must eventually return to the surface to breathe. But they can stay under a long time. Many pond turtles can normally stay submerged for a full day by taking oxygen directly out of the water through their skin.

A banded sea snake, or sea krait, spends its life in saltwater, feeding on fish. Unlike other sea snakes, though, kraits must come ashore to lay eggs.

The internal organs of snakes look a bit different from the organs of other animals. When snakes evolved their stretched-out bodies, they had to make certain adjustments to their organs as well as to their bones. In particular, their lungs changed shape. In most snakes, one lung—the right one—became longer and bigger. The left lung either shrank or disappeared completely. Other organs that normally come in pairs had to change as well. The kidneys, for example, which in other animals lie across from each other on opposite sides of the backbone, in snakes are staggered, with one squeezed farther down the body than the other.

THE SENSES

Reptile senses and sense organs vary with the orders. In general, reptiles have good eyesight. Crocodilians are among the best-sighted. Curiously, though, they do not see all that sharply underwater. They have a "third eyelid," called a nictitating membrane, that automatically closes over and protects their eyes as soon as they submerge. That membrane keeps them from focusing clearly below the surface.

Snakes are at the other end of the vision scale, and most see poorly. Snake eyes also differ from those of most other reptiles in that they are not protected by eyelids. (The presence or absence of lids is one way to distinguish a legless lizard from a snake.) A snake's eyes are instead covered by transparent scales, which are shed along with the rest of the skin.

Some reptiles also have a "third eye," just below the skin on top of the head. This extra sight organ is present in many lizards, and it is especially prominent in tuataras. The third eye is not really an eye, but it is similar. It consists of a disk of light-sensitive cells that are connected to an extension of the brain called the pineal body. The third eye does not form images. But it does allow the animal to gather information about light and dark, and it may help tell it when to hibernate.

Saltwater crocodiles of Papua New Guinea and Australia spend daytime hours in the warm sea, then come onto land at night to cool down.

All reptiles have ears, but not all are visible from the outside. And they do not all work equally well. Crocodilians and some lizards have external ear openings. Other lizards have eardrums that sit right at the surface of the head. Turtles have outer ears that lead down to eardrums, but on the outside the openings are covered over with scales. Snakes do not have ears or eardrums at all. Not surprisingly, they do not hear very well. Mostly, they hear through vibrations picked up by their jawbones.

Snakes make up for their lack of hearing with an extraordinary sense of smell. Partly they smell as we mammals do, with sensors lining the inside of their nostrils. But snakes have an additional way of detecting scents, through something called Jacobson's organ. This special structure (also called the vomeronasal organ) is located inside the roof of the mouth. Snakes use their tongues to pick up tiny scent particles from the air and transfer them to their Jacobson's organ through two tiny holes, or cavities, in the top of their mouth. Snakes receive most of their information about the world through their enhanced sense of smell. That is why they are always flicking out their forked tongues—they are picking up scent particles and bringing them back in for testing and identification. In fact, snake tongues are split into two points precisely to reach into the two tiny cavities that lead to Jacobson's organ.

JACOBSON'S ORGAN

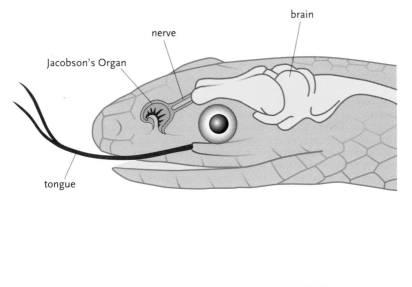

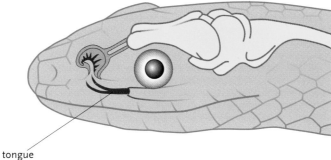

Some lizards always have forked tongues, for the same reason. Other lizards, and turtles too, have the same sensing organ but they do not rely on it as much and use their non-forked tongues for other, more familiar, purposes.

Some snakes also possess sensors for detecting heat, which they use to aid them in hunting. Boas and pythons have a row of heat sensors along their lips. The group of snakes known as pit vipers have a pair of heat sensors in two small pits on either side of their snout. These organs are so sensitive that they can not only detect the presence of a nearby warm animal, but also determine its precise location. Using its heat sensors alone, a pit viper can easily hunt down a meal in the dark.

GETTING AROUND

Most reptiles with legs walk in the familiar lizard mode, with limbs splayed out to the sides. Most lizards can walk and run quite quickly, but

Although it looks like a snake, the legless eastern glass lizard is exactly what its name suggests—a lizard (complete with the eyelids that a snake does not have).

because of their sprawled posture, they show a lot of side-to-side move-ment as they go. This is most exaggerated in species such as blind lizards and some skinks that have lost their limbs as they have adapted to a life underground or amidst dense vegetation. These lizards move as snakes do. Lizards that spend a lot of their time in the water, such as the Bornean earless lizard, also make use of this lateral, or side-to-side, motion to swim.

Tree-dwelling lizards, such as chameleons, often use tails that can grab on to branches as a fifth leg to help them climb. Chameleons also have specially adapted feet for life in the trees. Like tree-dwelling birds, they have some toes pointing forward and some backward. Working together, they allow the chameleon to get a firm grip.

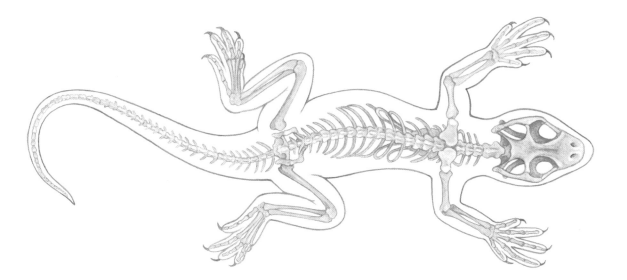

Lizard species with long tails use them to balance while walking or running. Some species even use their tails to grab or grasp things to keep their balance or to prevent falling.

A Southeast Asian flying dragon can glide between branches by spreading out its ribs and stretching the skin that runs from front legs to back.

A few lizards have bodies built for more unusual methods of travel. The flying dragons of Southeast Asia have a flap of skin that runs from front legs to back legs. The skin is attached to the lizards' unusually long ribs, which they are able to spread out to the sides. When they wish to move quickly from one branch to another high in their rain forest home, flying dragons can spread their ribs and glide, using their tails to help them steer.

Even more unusual is the ability of the basilisks to walk on water. When threatened these odd lizards rear up on their hind legs and run across the surface of a pond or stream, using their speed and the flaps of skin along their toes to keep them from sinking.

Snakes, with no legs, have developed four basic types of movement:

Rectilinear, or "straight," locomotion lets them travel in a straight

At high speed a basilisk can take an unusual escape route. It can actually run on water, thanks to specialized flaps of skin on its feet.

Depending upon the species, the number of vertebrae in a snake's backbone can range from 100 to more than 450. The structure of a snake's spine and vertebrae allow the animal to curl, twist, coil, and move.

line by using the broad scales on their underside. Moving them in succession, a snake can pull itself along the ground.

Serpentine, or lateral, locomotion is the typical side-to-side wavelike movement of a snake's body. As it bends its body into loops, the sides of the loops push against the ground (or the water, when the snake is swimming).

Sidewinding locomotion is used for crossing areas of loose sand. Basically, the snake moves forward and sideways at the same time, traveling roughly in a diagonal to the direction it is pointing. As the snake winds in the usual serpentine way, it lifts its head off the ground and throws the front part of its body sideways. The rest of the body follows.

Concertina locomotion is usually employed by tree-climbing snakes. While the scales on the underside of the front part of the snake grab on to rough bark, the rest of the body folds up behind the head in coils. Then the back end of the snake holds on while the head stretches forward to grab on to a new spot further up the tree.

Tree-dwelling snakes have a couple of other moves. Just like their lizard cousins, many are able to grasp branches with their tails. To span wider spaces, some Southeast Asian rain-forest snakes throw themselves

The same muscles that allow a kaleidoscope tree boa to hold on to a branch allow it to squeeze its prey until the animal can no longer breathe.

out of the treetops. At least three species of snakes engage in this wild behavior (all members of the genus *Chrysopelea*). They are called the paradise tree snake, the golden tree snake, and the twin-barred tree snake. To "fly," these snakes spread out their ribs, which are not joined at the front, and make the underside of their body cave in a bit to act as a parachute. By bending and wiggling their body in waves as they fall, these "flying" snakes can steer well enough to change direction in mid-flight.

Turtles are not nearly so adventurous, or so flexible. On land, they are notoriously slow and lumbering, and even in ponds and streams, many simply walk slowly along the bottom. Others, though, with long toes and webbed feet, swim quite gracefully, paddling with all four limbs. The true champions among the swimmers are the ocean-spanning sea turtles, with legs that have evolved into powerful flippers. Pulling themselves through the water with their front legs, and steering with their back legs, sea turtles can travel thousands of miles and reach speeds of 19 mph (30 kph).

Crocodilians also move quickly in the water, although they generally prefer not to. They are usually content to cruise calmly when swimming, powering themselves with snake-like waves of their long tail and using their feet to turn and brake. On land, their movement changes with the hardness of the ground. On mud or soft ground they crawl inelegantly on their bellies. When crossing firmer ground, however, they adopt a stance much more reminiscent of their extinct dinosaur relatives. Unlike other living reptiles, crocodilians are able to bring in their legs nearly directly under their bodies instead of splayed out to the sides. This "high walk" allows crocodiles to get their bellies well off the ground and to proceed at a stately pace of around 3 mph (4.8 kph).

That is not a blazing speed, but then, a 16- to 20-foot (5 to 6 m) alligator or crocodile has little reason to hurry. There are not many animals likely to be chasing it. A few crocodiles, however, who may occasionally have to make a fast getaway, do have one additional mode of locomotion: They race away in a gallop. Four different galloping crocodile species

Crocodilians like the American alligator use a "high walk" to travel on land. Unlike all other living reptiles, they can bring their legs in close to their body.

have been observed: The Australian freshwater crocodile, the New Guinea crocodile, the Nile crocodile, and the saltwater crocodile. When these animals are motoring over land at top speed, their hind feet push off the ground together, they leap through the air, land on their front feet, bring their hind feet forward, and push off again. This rabbit-like run can get a croc back to the safety of the water at a speed of around 10 mph (16 kph).

The Jackson's chameleon, like a number of other reptiles, gives birth to live young. Despite this photograph, however, chameleons offer their offspring little care.

CHAPTER THREE

Life Cycles

The typical reptile begins life as an egg, laid on land, in the company of dozens of other eggs. Upon hatching, the young animal must find food and shelter all on its own, or it will not survive. It will receive no care or protection from its parents or any other adult, and it will be hunted by predators of every animal type—by spiders, crabs, birds, mammals, and other reptiles, even of its own kind. Its chances of surviving that onslaught are, at best, poor. Still, if it lives through its childhood and adolescence, it may look forward to a long life. When it becomes an adult, it will find a member of the opposite sex and mate. But it will not stay with its mate and live as a family with its offspring. It will spend much of each day alone, lying in the warm sunlight. Once in a while it will eat. It will move quickly if it has to, but it will prefer to save its energy. Live slow, die old—that is its motto.

Unfortunately, although the paragraph above is true enough of reptiles in general, it describes very few reptiles in particular. Just as there is no single model for all reptile bodies, there is no single description that applies equally well to all reptile lives. Not all reptiles, for example, are born on land. Not all even hatch from eggs.

One-fifth of all snake species, including this eastern garter snake, do not lay eggs but instead give birth to large numbers of live young.

Twenty percent of snake species, for instance, do not lay eggs but give birth to live young. Among them are the common garter snake, boa constrictors, pipe snakes, and pit vipers. Live birth is frequently found among snakes living in cooler climates where the weather may not be dependable enough or long-lasting enough to incubate their eggs properly. A female snake that keeps the eggs inside her body until hatching can better control the incubation temperature. Many sea snakes, which spend their whole lives in the ocean, also bear live young. This handy evolutionary adaptation frees them from the need to come ashore.

It seems strange to talk about a reptile being "freed" from the land. After all, around 240 million years ago, the evolution of the amniotic egg "freed" reptiles from the need to return to the water. But some reptiles, like sea snakes, long ago gave up the advantages of living on land for the opportunities awaiting them in the ocean. For them, returning to land can be a serious burden.

This is certainly true for many sea turtles. All turtles lay their eggs on land, and for most this is not a problem. They live their entire lives within a short distance of their birthplace. But sea turtles span the oceans and travel far from their first home. Yet they are programmed by instinct to return to their birthplaces to lay their own eggs when the time comes. As a result, green sea turtles routinely travel nearly 3,000 miles (4,800 km) to build their nests.

Most turtles, whether sea- or land-based, build their nests and lay their eggs in the same way: the female digs a hole with her back feet, deposits the eggs, then covers them with sand, soil, or vegetation to keep them warm. The number of eggs in the nest varies, from one for the African tortoise to as many as 200 for some sea turtles. Loggerhead sea turtles may lay 6 "clutches," or groups, of 100 eggs each. Green sea turtles may lay as many as 11 clutches of that size. Turtles generally lay eggs every year, but sea turtles may lay eggs only every two or three years.

After the eggs are laid, the mother's involvement with her offspring is finished. Turtles neither watch over their nests nor guard and feed their young. The eggs, if undisturbed by an egg-loving snake, skunk,

Green sea turtles swim thousands of miles to lay their eggs on the beach where they themselves hatched. This behavior made them easy prey for early European sailors.

raccoon, or other predator, will take anywhere from 2 to 14 months to hatch. When they do, the young turtles must find shelter quickly.

Hatchlings are extremely vulnerable, and many are eaten in their first days. Sea turtle hatchlings are especially in danger. The nests they climb out of are always far enough up the beach to avoid damage from waves or tides. But, like their parents, the hatchlings are not built for life on land. They must travel down the beach to the sea as quickly and as unnoticeably as they can. During that brief journey, which often takes place at night, they are preyed upon by all manner of hungry diners, including birds, crabs, and a multitude of mammals. Even many of those turtles that make it to the water are eaten by fish. The life of a young sea turtle is very uncertain, at least until it grows too large for most predators to bother with. Most of a turtle's growth takes place in its first five years. Turtles that live that long are likely to make it to maturity—the age at which the turtle can itself reproduce. But few turtles reach that point. For sea turtles, the number is as low as a tenth of one percent—only one in a thousand sea turtle hatchlings ever has babies of its own. This predicament is not unusual for reptiles. Young snakes, lizards, and even baby crocodiles are especially tempting meals for predators. The reptile that lives to adulthood is a lucky reptile indeed.

Sea turtle hatchlings must get down the beach to the sea as quickly as possible. On land they are easy pickings for birds, crabs, and a variety of mammals.

Red rat snakes, also called corn snakes, lay up to thirty eggs in a single nest. Once all the eggs are laid, the mother will leave.

Like turtles, snakes pretty much lay their eggs and leave. A very few—chiefly some pythons and cobras—rest atop the eggs and protect them. Large pythons actually incubate the eggs, curling around them to keep them warm. Lizards, the snakes' close relatives, follow roughly the same pattern, laying eggs in groups of one to 50 and doing little else to ensure their survival. Like snakes, a number of lizards also give birth to live young. Among them are Jackson's chameleons, armadillo lizards, and many skinks.

A few lizards provide some care for their eggs. The Great Plains skink goes so far as to actively protect her newborns from the many predators who try to dine on them. Also, although the overwhelming number of lizards—like turtles and snakes—are basically loners, living, hunting, and caring only for themselves, some iguana hatchlings stay in groups. They often groom each other with their tongues, and sleep together on the branch of a tree.

To be fair, snakes and turtles sometimes gather in groups also. They often bask in the sun together, nest near each other, and hibernate together.

The large black iguanas of the Galapagos Islands are the only iguanas in the world that swim in salt-water and one of only two lizards that are strictly plant-eaters.

But they gather only because their numbers offer them greater protection or because the same basking or nesting spot appeals equally to them all. They do not really interact with one another to form a family or tribe.

Among the reptiles, that behavior is found only among crocodilians. Their lives are distinctly more complex than the lives of other reptiles and are much more similar to the lives of birds—to which they are actually more closely related. Crocodilians routinely spend far more time and energy taking care of their young and living as a family. And they routinely communicate with one another also, through sound, touch, smell, sight, and body posture.

Other reptiles "talk" to each other also, of course. Male and female snakes, lizards, and turtles all rely on smell or sight to varying degrees to find suitable mates. Some male lizards put on elaborate mating displays to impress females and intimidate other males. But none are as intent on communication as the crocodilians.

THE LIFE OF A CROCODILIAN

Generally, crocodiles and alligators and their kin dig or build nests out of soil or plant material, and lay 10 to 50 hard-shelled eggs inside. They cover over the eggs to keep them warm, then they leave. But they do not go far. The nests are built near a burrow or den where the female can rest. She does not stay on top of the nest, like a bird, but she does visit it frequently, and she tries to keep any interested egg-lovers away. In some species, the male also stays nearby to guard the nest.

Crocodilian chatter begins when the animals are still in the egg. After two to four months, when the eggs are ready to hatch, the babies begin tapping to each other and squealing out to their mother. The tapping seems to help make sure that all the babies hatch out at the same time. The calls bring on one or both parents to break open the nest. They help any of the babies that are having trouble cracking out of their shell by rolling the egg around gently in their mouths. Then they take all the hatchlings into their mouths to move them safely to shelter or to water to feed.

Much more than other reptiles, crocodilians take care of their young. Here a Nile crocodile carries her offspring in a basket that no predator is likely to touch.

The young remain with the adults for some time—a few months, in the case of Nile crocodiles, as long as two years in the case of American alligators. During that time the youngsters will frequently call out to one another to keep themselves together in a group. Adults too will call out, telling the youngsters to come near and other adults to keep their distance. (Adult crocodiles and alligators are often the most serious predators of other crocodiles and alligators.)

Other reptiles rarely get more vocal than an occasional hiss. Crocodilians not only hiss, they roar and grunt and bellow. In addition, they signal by slapping their tails and heads against the water or by clapping their great jaws. Through such signals, they try to keep their territories and families safe from intruders.

Despite all their efforts, the fate of many young crocodilians is the same as that of other reptiles. In all parts of the world there are always some animals that manage to sneak through and raid the crocodilians' nests. Among them are raccoons and opossums, skunks and foxes, rats and bears, and jackals and warthogs and large lizards.

Also, the nests can be flooded or dried out. In the end, perhaps a quarter of the eggs hatch. Of those that do, only a third to a half of the hatchlings live through their first few years. If they make it, though, they have a chance of living a quiet, unthreatened life of 20 to 40 years, depending on the species.

Reptiles often can enjoy long lives if they survive their early years. Some snakes and lizards live only half a dozen years or so, but many others live 20, 30, or even 50 or more years. Turtles are famously long-lived, with many species living 50, 60, or 70 years and some living 120, 150, and perhaps nearly 200 years. Tuataras too may live a century or more. But, then, they take a long time for everything. They lay their eggs only every 2 to 5 years. The eggs then take 11 to 15 months to hatch. After they do, young tuataras must grow for 10 or 12 years before they are ready to reproduce.

Reptile Life Spans

Common Name	Maximum Recorded Life Span (years)
Tuatara	77.0
Swamp turtle	11.7
Loggerhead turtle	33.0
Alligator snapping turtle	59.0
Aldabra tortoise	152.0
American blue lizard	2.3
Green basilisk	5.1
Tokay gecko	10.5
Green iguana	12.4
Gila monster	27.8
Common garter snake	10.0
Indian cobra	12.0
Western diamondback rattlesnake	25.8
Green anaconda	29.0
Common boa constrictor	38.8
False gharial (gavial)	14.3
Nile crocodile	15.0
American alligator	56.0

The Gila monster of the Southwest is one of only two lizard species that are poisonous, with venom powerful enough to kill a human.

CHAPTER FOUR

Habitat and Diet

AROUND THE WORLD

Reptiles live on every continent except Antarctica and in all the world's oceans. But when it comes to picking an ideal home, reptiles like it hot. As a result, the greatest number of reptiles live in the tropics and in the warmer regions of the temperate zones. Still, there are exceptions. A few hardy snakes and lizards live as far north as Norway and as far south as the tip of South America.

Turtles probably have the greatest range of any reptile, since sea turtles swim in oceans around the globe. Most other turtles are happy spending at least part of their time around marshes, streams, rivers, ponds, and lakes. In addition, there are some full-time landlubbers. These include the great tortoises, which make their slow way through grasslands, forests, and deserts.

Snakes and lizards live at higher elevations than turtles do. Some have made a home in the Himalayas, on mountains as high as 16,500 feet (5,000 m). They have also settled in the Rockies, the Andes, and the Alps. But the cold nighttime and winter temperatures of these spots make them less than perfect for cold-blooded creatures. Tropical forests and arid deserts are far more suitable territories.

Lizards are chiefly land and tree dwellers, although some spend time in freshwater ponds and streams, and one, the marine iguana, prefers to live in the ocean. Snakes have taken to saltwater more readily. A number of sea snakes live in the warm parts of the Indian and the Pacific oceans, around the equator. None, however, cruise the cold currents of the Atlantic. In addition, snakes have never managed to swim over to several large islands, including New Zealand and, famously, Ireland. But in the lands they do inhabit, they make use of every possible nook and niche, living on the ground, below the ground, and above it, in the trees.

Crocodilians are more picky. All of them live near water, but none really dwell in the oceans. They also are more determined to stay where it is warm. Almost all crocodilians are tropical animals. The northern

A South American dwarf caiman basks in the sun to raise its body temperature. These are the smallest of the crocodilians and feed mostly on fish.

exceptions are the American alligator, whose range stretches up the eastern coast of the United States as far as North Carolina, and the Chinese alligator, which lives in the lower parts of the Yangtze River. Several species also live below the tropics, in warmer parts of South America, Africa, and Australia.

The two species of tuatara have the most limited range of any reptile order. These ancient reptiles live only on 33 small islands around New Zealand. There they dwell quietly in forests around the shoreline, spending their days basking in the sun or resting in underground burrows and their nights hunting for food.

EATING

As a group, reptiles generally eat anything they can sink their teeth (or in the case of turtles, their horny, keratin-lined beaks) into. A few tortoises and lizards are herbivores, or plant-eaters. A fair number of others are omnivores, eating both plants and animals at different times of the year or at different points in their lives. Most reptiles, though, are dedicated carnivores, or meat-eaters. Precisely what they eat tends to vary with their size. Most, especially the larger ones, like the crocodiles, will gulp down anything they can get their mouths around.

Turtles

Turtles, not surprisingly, are not very active hunters. Those that live on land eat either plants or animals as slow as themselves, such as snails, insect larvae, or worms. Even the strong-swimming sea turtles go after slow or non-moving prey. Leatherbacks, for example, prefer jellyfish above all else. Hawksbill sea turtles feed mainly on sponges. Turtles that live in rivers, ponds, and lakes like to lie in ambush for their food rather than chase after it. Their usual method of attack is to conceal themselves on the sandy or stony bottom and wait for fish, insects, or frogs to come within reach. Then, with mouth open, they dart out their long necks and snatch their meal.

Many water-dwelling turtles use the "gape-and-suck" method for capturing tiny fish or tadpoles. They open their mouth and expand their throat, creating a suction that draws in water and anything swimming in it. The alligator snapping turtle has a more devious method of dining. On the end of its tongue this odd turtle has a bright-red wormlike "lure" that it wiggles back and forth to attract the attention of a passing fish. When the fish comes over to investigate, the snapper snaps and the fish becomes food.

Turtles do not have to eat often. They keep food in their digestive tracts for as long as four weeks, taking everything of value out of it. From their food they extract fat, which they store in their abdomen. This fat can easily sustain them during months of hibernation. Many turtles can probably go as long as a year without eating, if they must.

By wiggling a red "lure" that grows on the end of its tongue, an alligator snapping turtle entices fish to come toward its mouth.

Reptiles in Winter

Because reptiles depend on the external environment for their internal warmth, they are not able to function well in the cold. This, for the most part, has kept reptiles residents of warmer climates. But many turtles, snakes, and lizards that have spread to cooler regions manage to live through winters by hibernating. Like such mammals as bats, chipmunks, and groundhogs, once the temperature drops below a certain point, these reptiles find some protected rock crevice, underground den, or mud hole, shut their bodies down, and wait for spring. Among the many hibernating reptiles are rattlesnakes and garter snakes, sagebrush lizards and collared lizards, and a variety of pond and river turtles.

Hibernation in reptiles is not quite the same as in mammals. As temperatures cool, ectothermic (cold-blooded) animals naturally slow down. When the outside temperature is no longer high enough for reptiles to move about freely, they enter a state of "torpor," or sluggishness, during which all their internal processes, such as circulation and respiration, slow down dramatically. Digestion stops completely. The food they have eaten before hibernating has been turned into fat, which will sustain them until they wake. Heartbeat may slow to a single beat every few minutes. Breathing must continue, but a reptile needs much less oxygen than a mammal to survive. Many pond turtles are able to hibernate underwater for months because they can "breathe" without using their lungs. They can take oxygen directly out of the water through the skin in their mouths and nostrils. They also seem to be able to take in oxygen through the skin of their cloacas—an unusual way to breathe, certainly, but apparently a very effective one.

Lizards

Among the lizards, only two species are really herbivores, although a number of lizards do eat fruit along with their main meat course. The most interesting plant eaters are the marine iguanas of the Galapagos Islands. These large web-footed lizards, which grow more than 5 feet (1.5 m) long, dive as deep as 50 feet (15 m) to munch on kelp and sea plants, and they are often seen eating algae off of rocks.

Most lizards, though, are meat-eaters, and rather small—around 3 to 8 inches (7.5 to 20 cm) long. At that size, the most common appropriate prey animals are insects and spiders. The large supply of these six- and eight-footed animals is what sustains great numbers of four-footed ones. The main mode of lizard attack is to move swiftly and snatch an insect in its jaws. African chameleons, however, snag insects on the sticky tips of their amazingly long tongues (which can stretch the length of the lizard itself).

A Parson's chameleon attacks an unwary insect with a lightning-fast tongue as long as its entire body. The tip of the tongue is coated with sticky mucus.

On a few Indonesian islands, a reptile still rules as top predator. The Komodo dragon grows up to 10 feet (3 m) long and weighs as much as 300 pounds (136 kg).

Larger lizards have a wider diet. The largest of all lizards, the 10-foot (3 m) Komodo dragons of Indonesia, will eat just about anything, dead or alive, and are as happy to be scavengers as hunters. On their island homes they are the top predators, easily able to bring down goats, pigs, deer, and even water buffalo. That is no small feat—a water buffalo may weigh 10 or 15 times more than a 300-pound (136 kg) dragon.

Komodo dragons are anything but boring hunters. Their favored method of attacking large prey is to ambush the animal and quickly snatch at it with their large powerful jaws and sharp, serrated teeth. They rip out a large chunk of flesh from the animal's belly or hindquarters, then simply wait for the animal to collapse from shock or loss of blood. The bites are so severe that few animals, once attacked, ever escape. Even those that at first get away soon die. The mouth of the dragon is a notorious breeding ground for bacteria, and the wounds it inflicts are infected quickly.

In a way, the dragon's bacteria-infested saliva acts as slow-acting venom, or poison, although these lizards are not truly poisonous. In fact, there are only two species of poisonous lizards: the beaded lizard of Mexico and the related Gila monster, which lives in the deserts of northern Mexico and the southwestern United States. The beaded lizard, at a maximum length of just over 3 feet (1 m), is the larger of the two. The Gila monster is about half its size. Both have glands in their lower jaw that produce a powerful venom able to paralyze the muscles of any animal injected with it, stopping its heart and lungs. Both can kill something even as large as a human, though fatal attacks on people are rare.

Snakes

The masters of poison among reptiles, of course, are the snakes. Although all snakes are eaters of other animals, not all of them use venom to kill. Out of the nearly 3,000 species of snakes, perhaps a quarter are venomous. Of these, fewer than 300 species are potentially harmful to humans. Still, each year a lot of people—50,000 to 100,000—die from snakebites, most of them inflicted by members of just 25 species, among them rattlesnakes, moccasins, cobras, mambas, asps, and adders. Venomous snakes have enlarged teeth, called fangs, with a hollow channel inside, through which the venom flows. The glands that produce the venom are usually in the head, behind the eyes. To make room for these glands, most venomous snakes have enlarged, triangular heads.

All snakes, from the 6-inch (15 cm) Braminy blind snake to the 30-foot (9 m) anaconda, follow one of two hunting methods. They either actively seek out their prey, or they lie in ambush. Snakes that feed mainly on small, slow-moving prey, such as insects, can afford to go after them. Larger snakes that feed on larger prey are nearly always ambushers.

Snakes eat a huge variety of animals, including fish, frogs, lizards, birds, other snakes, and mammals. The largest snakes eat quite large

This dromicus snake begins a meal of lava lizard in typical fashion, swallowing the prey head first so that limbs can fold in and not get stuck in the snake's throat.

animals. An African rock python, for example, is able to feast on an antelope as big as an impala. Most snakes are not at all picky about their food, eating anything in the proper size range. But some are specialists. Tiny thread snakes dine only on termites. Hook-nosed snakes snack only on spiders. Some snakes have a special diet of eggs.

How snakes capture their prey varies. Snakes that eat small animals simply grab them in their jaws. Snakes attacking larger animals that can fight back must immobilize or kill them first. They do this either by poison, or suffocation. This last method is the one used by boa constrictors, pythons, and anacondas. They first grab the prey animal in their mouth, then coil around it, drawing their body tighter and tighter until the animal can no longer breathe.

Snakes have no way of taking their food in small pieces, so they must swallow it whole. Because the animals they eat are often large, the snakes must take some precautions. For example, they generally eat animals head first to allow arms and legs to fold in close to the body and keep them from getting stuck on the way down.

They also have some physical adaptations that allow them to swallow their supersize meals. First, their jaws are only loosely attached to each other and to the skull, so they can open very wide to surround an animal larger than the snake's head. Snakes can also move the left and right sides of their jaws separately—the bones are not joined in front, as ours are—to "walk" in a mouthful of prey and push it down their throat. Second, the snake's entire body can stretch to allow a large animal to move through. Even the ribs can stretch apart to make room for a passing feast. Third, snake venom and snake saliva are filled with digestive fluids that help break down the food long before it gets to the stomach. Like turtles and other reptiles, snakes can make their meals last a long time. They can easily go weeks or months between meals, and they can fast for a year if they must.

Crocodilians

Crocodilians share many of the eating habits of other reptiles. They too prefer to lie in ambush rather than chase down prey. They do not chew their food and either swallow animals whole or tear off large chunks of them. And they have powerful digestive systems that make the most of whatever they swallow—crocodilians can digest nearly every part of any animal, including all the bones. Finally, like other reptiles, crocodilians can fast for a very long time. A large crocodile, living off its stores of fat, could go without a meal for an astonishing two years.

Alligators and crocodiles can mount an impressive attack on their prey. Although they spend their energy quickly, they can put on a tremendous burst of speed for a short distance, rushing up the shore for several yards (or meters) to surprise an animal before it has time to react. They can also leap out of the water as high as 5 feet (1.5 m) to grab a passing bird or an animal on a riverbank.

Crocodilians usually kill their larger prey by drowning it, holding it underwater in their powerful jaws until it stops struggling. Sometimes, with very large prey—a zebra, for example—they will tear the animal into pieces before gulping it down. One way they do this is by grabbing a leg, then twirling around underwater until the limb breaks free. At other times they work cooperatively with others of their kind, treating the prey like a rope in a tug of war—very sophisticated and unusual behavior for reptiles.

Generally, crocodilians are very open-minded about diet, though narrow-snouted species, like the gharial, are fish specialists. But other broad-snouted crocodilians will eat anything. Most in fact eat everything—as hatchlings, they start out with small prey like insects, then move up to tadpoles, frogs, crabs, and small fish as they grow. Larger crocodilians progress to whatever large prey is available in their part of the world: otters, pigs, deer, horses, water buffalo, wildebeest, elephants—nothing is off-limits, not even the occasional human.

A Nile crocodile can charge up a riverbank fast enough to grab a wildebeest before it can flee. Usually it will then drag its prey back into the water to drown it.

Some reptile defenses are more bluff than bite. The frilled lizard inflates its body and spreads its collar to look far more fierce than it is.

Surviving the Present, and the Future

Reptiles themselves are often prey as well as predators, of course. But like all animals, they have developed ways to keep themselves out of the stomachs of others.

For a few, size and might alone are sufficient. Animals attacking a large crocodile or alligator are met with huge teeth, powerful jaws, a vicious tail, sharp claws, and an impenetrable coat of bony armor. Although a very large snake may kill a medium-size caiman, in the wild, the largest crocodilians are killed only by something as large as an elephant or hippo protecting its family against attack.

Turtles generally rely on their armored shells for protection. Some, when threatened, also discharge a strong, foul-smelling substance from glands on their sides. This so-called musk is off-putting enough to drive away many predators, including people. The champion of bad-smelling turtles is known as the stinkpot turtle, and its talent is celebrated in its species name: *oderatus*. Not all turtles are so passive in their defense. Snapping turtles have very strong and sharp jaws and are very aggressive.

Like nearly all animals, reptiles prefer to meet threats by running away if they can, rather than fighting. So most snakes and lizards, no matter how large, immediately respond to a threat by scurrying or slithering into the nearest underbrush, burrow, or rock crevice, or by climbing up a tree. If escape is not possible, some snakes and lizards just play dead, going so far as to flop over on their backs and let their tongues hang out. Surprisingly, the ruse sometimes works. Some predators will attack only live prey, and they do not respond to a motionless animal.

Alternatively, some lizards and snakes take the opposite approach and try to make themselves look fierce. The Australian frilled lizard is a master at this game. It fans out the large collar of skin around its head and inflates its body to make itself appear much larger and more dangerous than it really is. The blue-tongued skink puts on a threat display by opening its mouth and hissing while proudly showing its attacker its oddly

colored tongue. Apparently, this disconcerts some diners. So does the unusual behavior of the horned lizard of the Southwest. It faces down predators by squirting blood at them from its eyes. This seems to stop foxes and coyotes (although why an animal intent on munching a raw lizard would be put off by a little blood is not clear).

Mexican beaded lizards and Gila monsters also open their mouths and hiss, but their venom makes their display much more than an empty threat. This is true also of the hissing displays of

A most unusual defense is deployed by the horned lizard, which squirts blood from its eyes to confuse and repel a predator.

An Indian cobra uses a threatening display to scare off an Indian gray mongoose looking for a meal.

cobras and the noisy warnings of rattlesnakes. All venomous snakes can mount a serious defense if cornered.

Naturally, the best situation is for snakes and lizards not to be attacked in the first place. Many poisonous snakes, such as coral snakes, have bodies decorated with bright bands of red, yellow, and black. Like the black and yellow stripes of wasps and bees, these colors alert would-be predators to stay away. This works well enough that a number of non-poisonous snakes, such as milk snakes, have evolved very similar markings to fool predators into thinking that they too are poisonous.

In the Costa Rican rain forest, a venomous eyelash viper relies on camouflage more for hunting than protection as it waits to ambush a small mammal, lizard, or frog.

A more common method of avoiding predators is by concealment. Most snakes and lizards are colored and patterned to blend in with the natural background of dirt, leaves, twigs, or rocks. Chameleons can change their color as needed, with some species running the spectrum from orange to yellow to blue-green.

ADAPTING FOR SURVIVAL

As a group, reptiles have some other characteristics, in both their bodies and their behavior, that have helped them through the ages. The benefits of some are as obvious as the benefits of camouflage coloring. The benefits of others, though, are much less clear.

In the first category are those changes that allowed the reptiles' ancestors to move from water to land in the first place, and to survive in the often dry, hot environments that were available for settlement. Among these is the animals' ability to conserve water. Reptiles lose much less water than mammals do. They do not perspire and they do not produce liquid waste; their urine comes out in a solid form. Waste products from the kidneys are sent to the cloaca, where any water is absorbed back into the body. This ability to recycle water, combined with their low food requirements, allows them to thrive in arid, sparse deserts that many other animals find intolerable.

The point of another reptile adaptation is not so obvious. Some reptiles have developed a very odd way of producing babies. In nearly all other animals, the sex of a baby—whether it is a male or a female—is decided by the instructions it carries in its cells. However, among crocodilians, tuataras, and most turtles, the sex of their offspring is decided by the temperature in the nest while the eggs are incubating. In other words, when the eggs are laid they can produce either males or females. What eventually hatches out from them depends only on how warm or cool they get.

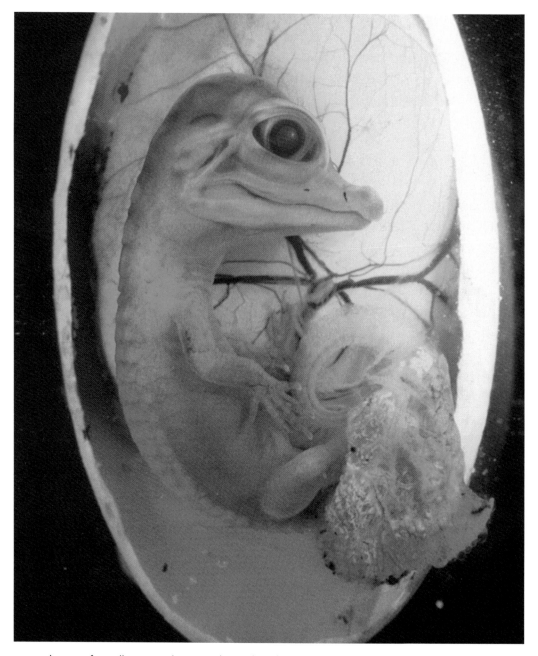

The sex of an alligator is determined not when the egg is fertilized but by how warm or cool the egg is in the nest during a critical period of development.

Small temperature differences, even within a single nest, can have big effects. In crocodiles, for example, eggs incubated between 89 and 92 degrees Fahrenheit (32 to 33 degrees C) will become males. Eggs kept just a touch warmer or cooler will become females. The details are different for tuataras and turtles, with different temperature ranges producing different results. Usually, all the eggs in a single nest will produce all males or all females. But the mechanism is so sensitive that occasionally temperature differences between regions of the nest will produce females, say, from the top eggs and males from the bottom.

Why this strange method of reproduction evolved is something of a mystery. But it apparently has worked well enough to ensure these reptiles' survival up to the present. So, naturally, have all the other reptile adaptations. With bodies built for patience and endurance, today's reptiles have prospered for many tens of millions of years. They have survived the shifting of continents, the coming and going of ice ages, and the impact of asteroids. Yet they may not be able to withstand the impact of humans much longer.

THE HUMAN THREAT

Throughout the past century, humans have made life increasingly difficult for reptiles. We have thinned their numbers dramatically, reduced their great variety, and severely limited their future prospects. We have butchered many millions of reptiles for their meat and skins, slaughtered many others out of fear or prejudice, poisoned the waterways they swim in, and taken away the land and the forests they need for their homes. Some people are trying to stop and even reverse the damage, but whether their efforts can be successful is not yet known.

Turtles of all kinds, for example, are in danger. Of the 302 turtle species, at least one-third, and maybe as many as one-half, face a serious threat of extinction. The crisis for freshwater turtles is particularly severe

Researchers keep track of eggs in a loggerhead turtle's nest. Many places around the world have laws protecting endangered sea turtles, their nests, eggs, and hatchlings.

in Asia, where turtles have long been hunted both for food and for use in traditional medicines. They are still being collected in huge numbers throughout the continent.

Sea turtles are in trouble the world over. Their problems actually began three centuries ago, when seafaring European explorers first discovered the animals' great value as food. Sea turtles are large, and they can go for long periods without food or water. They are also easy to catch, since they always return to the same beaches to lay their eggs. So they were very easy and profitable animals for ships to capture and carry back to Europe live. There they were a high-priced delicacy. Millions were turned into soup. Hawksbill sea turtles had the additional misfortune of a richly colored hard shell that was prized for its use in "tortoiseshell" jewelry.

Today, all seven species of sea turtles are in danger. By some estimates, one out of every three sea turtles ends up being killed for food by humans. Among the most threatened is the leatherback, the world's largest turtle. It routinely grows to be 96 inches (244 cm) long, if it reaches adulthood. But over the past quarter-century, fewer and fewer leatherbacks are making it to maturity. By some estimates, there are 70 percent fewer leatherbacks than there were a generation ago. There may be no more than 20,000 of them left in the seas.

The situation is similar for snakes, lizards, and crocodilians, although the details differ. All of them have been hunted for their skins, which have been put to use in shoes, handbags, and other fashion items. Snakes and lizards have long been hunted as food in many parts of the world, and they still are. In some areas, humans are among the major predators of crocodile and turtle eggs as well. Many sea turtles are killed accidentally, caught in the large nets of modern deep-sea fishing fleets. Many snakes, meanwhile,

Snakes and turtle skins can be seen for sale throughout Asia, where they are often used as ingredients in traditional medicines.

The rare "false" gharial of Malaysia has become extremely endangered, despite laws to protect it, as its habitat has been destroyed or turned into farmland.

especially rattlesnakes, are killed on purpose—out of a mistaken notion of the dangers they pose to humans, out of revulsion, or just for "sport." Some rare lizards, meanwhile, have been collected as pets.

But, by far, the biggest problem for reptiles of all sorts is the destruction of their natural habitat. They are all rapidly losing ground—literally— as more and more land is cleared, drained, or otherwise remade for farms, ranches, homes, or resorts. The damage comes in many forms. Sometimes it is direct, as when part of a Central American rain forest is burned. The great rain forests of the tropics are the natural homes for many animal species, including reptiles, and their loss is devastating. Undoubtedly, as we lose the rain forests, we forever lose species of lizards and snakes that we did not even know existed.

Rain forests are not the only disappearing habitat. Woods, fields, and marshes everywhere are being eaten up. Even deserts are being remade, areas where until now reptiles have always been able to dwell undisturbed. Today, cities throughout the American West and Southwest

The Antiguan racer is often called the world's rarest snake. In the wild, these snakes can only be found on Great Bird Island, located off the coast of Antigua in the Caribbean Sea.

are expanding rapidly. So are the highways and the traffic that link those cities. That growth, directly or indirectly, affects reptile populations.

Some indirect damage comes from animals that arrive along with the homes and farms and ranches, animals that are not native to the area. Pigs, goats, dogs, cats, and rats can destroy an enormous number of eggs and nests and radically change a landscape. Such animals have been especially destructive to island habitats, where the native reptiles have little room for escape.

Other indirect dangers come from buildings near nesting areas of turtles and crocodilians. By creating unnatural shaded or cleared areas, buildings can allow in more or less sunlight and change the temperature of the soil in which the eggs are incubating. Even a slight change could result in a lopsided number of males or females being born. Normally, odd occurrences like this would balance out over time. But in populations that are already threatened, changes of these sorts could be serious.

The situation faced by alligators and crocodiles may be the most instructive for us. Actually, some of these creatures, such as the American alligator, are doing just fine—after being pushed to the brink of extinction. Not long ago, alligators in the United States were hunted mercilessly for their skins. Today they and their habitats are fully protected by law, and

Laws can sometimes work to save threatened reptiles. In New Zealand, the tuatara—the last survivor of an ancient order of reptiles—is now actually doing well.

alligator ranches have been established to grow alligators for human use. Other countries around the world, such as Australia, have taken similar steps, and some crocodilian populations have bounced back.

But not all, and not everywhere. Despite the successes of a few species, as a group crocodilians may be the most embattled animal order on Earth. One half of all species are considered endangered. The range and numbers of the Chinese alligator, for instance, has continued to shrink every year. No matter what measures the Chinese government may take at this point, the Chinese alligator may already be doomed to extinction in the wild.

Strangely, the safest group of reptiles in the world today may well be the tuataras. These secretive animals, the last surviving members of the order Rhynchocephalia, have been reduced to a total population of perhaps 60,000 animals living on a few dozen small islands around New Zealand. Yet their future looks bright. They and their island homes are completely protected by the New Zealand government. There is nothing to prevent any individual tuatara from living out its century-long life, just as its ancestors did tens of millions of years ago—before there was a single human in the world to threaten them.

adaptation—A change in an organism that allows it to function better in its environment.

amniote—An animal that lays an amniotic egg; also, the descendants of such an animal. All reptiles, birds, and mammals are amniotes.

amniotic egg—A shell-covered egg, such as one laid by a reptile or bird, that does not need to be laid in the water; inside the egg, the embryo is enclosed in a fluid-filled sac.

bask—To lie in the sun and absorb heat.

bridge—The bony connection on the side of a turtle between the top and bottom halves of its shell.

carapace—The top half of a turtle's shell.

class—A level of biological classification above order and below phylum; all reptiles belong to the class Reptilia.

clutch—A single group of eggs.

ectothermic—Refers to an animal that does not maintain a constant internal temperature; ectothermic, or cold-blooded, animals get their heat from the environment.

embryo—A developing organism, such as a young reptile still in the egg.

endothermic—Refers to an animal that produces heat from food to maintain its internal body temperature at a constant level.

extinction—The final disappearance of all members of a species.

family—A level of classification above genus and below order; both the American alligator and the Chinese alligator, for example, belong to the family Alligatoridae.

gland—An organ in the body that produces a particular type of chemical substance.

ichthyosaur—An extinct fish-shaped or dolphin-shaped reptile that lived in the seas during the age of the dinosaurs.

Jacobson's organ—An organ in some animals that allows them to sense chemical or scent particles picked up from the air; also called the vomeronasal organ.

keratin—A protein that, in reptiles, makes up the tough scales of their skin; in other animals it forms horns and fingernails, as well as hair.

kingdom—The highest level of classification; all animals are gathered into the kingdom Animalia, one of the five kingdoms that contain all living things.

membrane—A thin, skin-like sheet of tissue.

musk—A strong-smelling substance produced by some animals, such as turtles.

nictitating membrane—A protective "third eyelid" that moves sideways across the eye.

order—A high taxonomic level, below the level of class and above family and genus; there are four living orders of reptiles.

organism—An individual living thing; a single plant or animal.

osteoderm— A small plate of bone embedded in the skin of some reptiles.

phylum—A very high level of classification, right below that of kingdom.

pineal body—An extension of the brain that in some reptiles connects to the "third eye," an organ used for sensing light and dark.

plastron—The bottom half of a turtle's shell.

plesiosaur—One of a group of extinct sea-going reptiles that had flipper-like limbs and, often, very long necks.

predator—An animal that kills other animals for food.

prey—An animal that is hunted and killed by another animal.

rain forest—A forest that gets at least 100 inches (254 cm) of rainfall each year; tropical rain forests have the greatest variety of animal and plant species on the planet.

scale—In a reptile, a tough, flat section of skin.

scute—An enlarged scale, such as found in the shell of a turtle or on the back of a crocodile.

species—The basic unit of classification that defines a "specific" type of animal or plant; all humans belong to the single species *Homo sapiens.*

taxon—Any one of the levels of biological classification, such as species or class.

taxonomy—The science of biological classification.

tetrapod—An animal that has, or whose ancestors had, four limbs; all reptiles, including snakes, are tetrapods, as are all amphibians, birds, and mammals.

venom—Poison produced by specialized glands in an animal such as a snake or one of two species of lizard.

vertebra—One of the bones of the spine.

ORDER	TESTUDINES Turtles—302 species	CROCODYLIA	
SUBORDER			**SAURIA** **Lizards—4,675 species**

FAMILY			
	Chelydridae (snapping turtles) Emydidae (pond turtles, box turtles, water turtles) Testudinidae (tortoises) Bataguridae (Asian river turtles, leaf and roofed turtles, Asian box turtles) Carettochelyidae (pignose turtles) Trionychidae (softshell turtles) Dermatemydidae (river turtles) Kinosternidae (mud and musk turtles) Cheloniidae (sea turtles) Dermochelyidae (leatherback turtles) Chelidae (Austro-American sideneck turtles) Pelomedusidae (Afro-American sideneck turtles) Podocnemididae (Madagascan big-headed turtles, American sideneck river turtles)	Crocodylidae (crocodiles—14 species) Alligatoridae (alligators and caimans— 8 species) Gavialidae (gharials—1 species) *[Sometimes all genera are listed within the single family Crocodylidae]*	Agamidae (agamas) Chamaeleonidae (chameleons) Iguanidae (iguanas) Gekkonidae (geckoes) Pygopodidae (legless lizards) Dibamidae (blind lizards) Cordylidae (spinytail lizards) Gerrhosauridae (plated lizards) Gymnophthalmidae (spectacled lizards) Teiidae (whiptails, tegus) Lacertidae (lacertids, wall lizards) Scincidae (skinks) Xantusiidae (night lizards) Anguidae (glass lizards, alligator lizards, lateral fold lizards) Anniellidae (American legless lizards) Xenosauridae (knob-scaled lizards) Helodermatidae (Gila monsters) Varanidae (monitor lizards) Lanthanotidae (earless monitor lizards)

FAMILY TREE

CLASS REPTILIA

SQUAMATA

RHYNCHOCEPHALIA
Tuataras—2 species

AMPHISBAENIA
Worm-lizards—160 species

SERPENTES
Snakes—2,940 species

Amphisbaenidae (worm-lizards)
Trogonophidae
  (shorthead worm-lizards)
Bipedidae
  (two-legged worm-lizards)
Rhineuridae
  (Florida worm-lizard)

Anomalepidae
  (dawn blind snakes)
Typhlopidae (blind snakes)
Leptotyphlopidae
  (slender blind snakes)
Aniliidae (pipe snakes)
Anomochilidae
  (dwarf pipe snakes)
Boidae (boas, pythons)
Bolyeridae
  (round island boas)
Cylindrophiidae
  (Asian pipe snakes)
Loxocemidae
  (Mexican burrowing pythons)
Tropidophiidae (dwarf boas)
Uropeltidae
  (shield-tail snakes)
Xenopeltidae
  (sunbeam snakes)
Acrochordidae (file snakes)
Atractaspididae (mole vipers)
Colubridae (colubrids)
Elapidae
  (cobras, kraits, coral snakes)
Hydrophiidae (sea snakes)
Viperidae
  (vipers, pit vipers)

Sphenodontidae

F U R T H E R   R E A D I N G

Ernst, Carl H. and George Zug. *Snakes in Question: The Smithsonian Answer Book.* Washington, D.C.: Smithsonian Institution Press, 1996.

Lamar, William W., Bill Love, et al. *The World's Most Spectacular Reptiles & Amphibians.* Tampa, FL: World Publications, 1997.

Orenstein, Ronald. *Turtles, Tortoises and Terrapins: Survivors in Armor.* Buffalo, NY: Firefly Books, 2001.

Perrine, Doug. *Sea Turtles of the World* (Worldlife Discovery Guides). Stillwater, MN: Voyageur Press, 2003.

W E B   S I T E S

Tuataras

Terra Nature
http://www.terranature.org/tuatara.htm

Crocodilians

CROCODILIANS: Natural History & Conservation (hosted by Florida Museum of Natural History)
http://www.crocodilian.com

Sea turtles

The Caribbean Conservation Corporation
http://www.cccturtle.org/ccctmp.htm

Turtle Trax
http://www.turtles.org/

Extinct sea-going reptiles (and others)

Oceans of Kansas Paleontology
http://www.oceansofkansas.com/

Warm- and cold-blooded animals

Infrared Zoo Gallery
http://coolcosmos.ipac.caltech.edu/image_galleries/ir_zoo/

BIBLIOGRAPHY

The following sources provided helpful information or background:

Alderton, David. *Turtles & Tortoises of the World*. New York: Facts on File, 1988.

Alexander, R. McNeill. *Dynamics of Dinosaurs and Other Extinct Giants*. New York: Columbia University Press, 1989.

Ball, Philip. "Wriggle Makes Flying Snakes Glide." Nature Science Update, June 6, 2003. http://www.nature.com/nsu/030602/030602-14.html

Carey, James R. and Debra S. Judge. *Odense Monographs on Population Aging 8: Longevity Records: Life Spans of Mammals, Birds, Amphibians, Reptiles, and Fish*. Denmark: Odense University Press. Accessed through Max Planck Institute for Demographic Research: http://www.demogr.mpg.de/longevityrecords/0403.htm

Diamond, Jared. "The Evolution of the Dragon." *Discover*, December 1992.

Fortey, Richard. *Life: A Natural History of the First Four Billion Years of Life on Earth*. New York: Alfred A. Knopf, 1998.

Gould, Stephen Jay, ed., *The Book of Life: An Illustrated History of the Evolution of Life on Earth*. New York: W. W. Norton & Company, 1993.

Gould, Stephen Jay. *Eight Little Piggies*. New York: W. W. Norton & Company, 1993.

—- *Bully for Brontosaurus.* New York: W. W. Norton & Company, 1991.

Halliday, Tim and Kraig Adler, eds. *Firefly Encyclopedia of Reptiles and Amphibians.* Buffalo, NY: Firefly Books, 2002.

Mattison, Chris. *Snakes of the World.* New York: Facts on File, 1986.

McGowan, Chris. *Diatoms to Dinosaurs: The Size and Scale of Living Things.* Washington, D.C.: Island Press, 1994.

Ross, Charles A., ed. *Crocodiles and Alligators.* New York: Facts on File, 1989.

Uetz, Peter, ed. European Molecular Biology Laboratory Reptile Database. http://www.reptile-database.org/

Wellnhofer, Peter. *The Illustrated Encyclopedia of Pterosaurs.* New York: Crescent Books, 1991.

Whitfield, John. "Fishing Kills a Third of Turtles." Nature Science Update, November 10, 2003. http://www.nature.com/nsu/031103/031103-17.html

Zug, George R. *Herpetology: An Introductory Biology of Amphibians and Reptiles.* San Diego: Academic Press, 1993.

I N D E X

Page numbers in **boldface** are illustrations and charts.

Marc Zabludoff, former editor in chief of *Discover* magazine, has been involved in communicating science to the public for more than two decades. He has written two other books in this series for Marshall Cavendish, on insects and on the kingdom of life made up of the chiefly microscopic—and largely unknown—organisms known as protoctists. His books for the AnimalWays series include *Spiders* and future works on beetles and monkeys. Zabludoff lives in New York City with his wife and daughter.